Gabriel Fauré

REQUIEM

IN FULL SCORE

DOVER PUBLICATIONS, INC., NEW YORK

This Dover edition, first published in 1992,
is a republication of the edition originally published
by J. Hamelle, Paris, in 1900.
Translations of the texts have been added.

Manufactured in the United States of America
Dover Publications, Inc.
31 East 2nd Street
Mineola, N.Y. 11501

Library of Congress Cataloging-in-Publication Data

Fauré, Gabriel, 1845–1924.
[Requiem, op. 48, D minor]
Requiem / Gabriel Fauré.—In full score.
1 score.
For solo voices (SBar), chorus (SATB), and orchestra.
Latin words, also printed as text with English translations.
Reprint. Originally published: Paris : J. Hamelle, 1900.
ISBN 0-486-27155-2
1. Requiems—Scores.
M2010.F26 op. 48 1992 92-19009
CIP
M

Contents

Texts and Translations

Introit and Kyrie

Requiem aeternam dona eis, Domine, et lux perpetua luceat eis. Te decet hymnus, Deus, in Sion, et tibi reddetur votum in Jerusalem. Exaudi orationem meam; ad te omnis caro veniet. Kyrie eleison. Christe eleison.

Introit and Kyrie

Grant them eternal rest, Lord, and may perpetual light shine upon them. A hymn, O God, becometh thee in Sion, and a vow shall be paid to thee in Jerusalem. Hear my prayer; to thee all flesh shall come. Lord, have mercy. Christ, have mercy.

Offertory

O Domine Jesu Christe, rex gloriae, libera animas defunctorum de poenis inferni, et de profundo lacu. Libera animas defunctorum de ore leonis, ne absorbeat Tartarus, ne cadant in obscurum. Hostias et preces tibi, Domine, laudis offerimus, tu suscipe pro animabus illis, quarum hodie memoriam facimus. Fac eas, Domine, de morte transire ad vitam. Quam olim Abrahae promisisti, et semini ejus.

Offertory

O Lord Jesus Christ, king of glory, deliver the souls of the dead from the pains of hell, and from the deep lake; deliver the souls of the dead from the lion's mouth; let not Tartarus swallow them, nor let them fall into darkness. We offer prayers and sacrifices to thee, O Lord, together with praise; receive them in behalf of those souls whom we this day commemorate. Grant, O Lord, that they pass from death to life, as thou didst promise to Abraham and to his seed.

Sanctus

Sanctus, Sanctus, Sanctus, Dominus Deus Sabaoth. Pleni sunt coeli et terra gloria tua. Hosanna in excelsis.

Sanctus

Holy, Holy, Holy, Lord God of Hosts. Heaven and earth are full of thy glory. Hosanna in the highest.

Pie Jesu

Pie Jesu Domine, dona eis requiem, sempiternam requiem.

Pie Jesu

Blessed Lord Jesus, grant them rest, everlasting rest.

Agnus Dei

Agnus Dei, qui tollis peccata mundi, dona eis requiem, sempiternam requiem. Lux aeterna luceat eis, Domine, cum sanctis tuis in aeternum, quia pius es. Requiem aeternam dona eis, Domine, et lux perpetua luceat eis.

Agnus Dei

Lamb of God, who takest away the sins of the world, grant them rest, everlasting rest. May eternal light shine upon them, Lord, with thy saints in eternity, for thou art merciful. Grant them eternal rest, Lord, and may perpetual light shine upon them.

Libera me

Libera me, Domine, de morte aeterna, in die illa tremenda, quando coeli movendi sunt et terra. Dum veneris judicare saeculum per ignem. Tremens factus sum ego, et timeo, dum discussio venerit, atque ventura ira. Dies illa, dies irae, calamitatis et miseriae. Dies illa, dies magna et amara valde. Requiem aeternam dona eis, Domine, et lux perpetua luceat eis.

In paradisum

In paradisum deducant angeli, in tuo adventu suscipiant te martyres, et perducant te in civitatem sanctam Jerusalem. Chorus angelorum te suscipiat, et cum Lazaro quondam paupere aeternam habeas requiem.

Libera me

Deliver me, Lord, from eternal death, in that awful day when heaven and earth shall be moved, when thou shalt come to judge the world by fire. Full of terror am I, and I fear the trial and the wrath to come. That day shall be a day of wrath, of calamity and misery. That day shall be a mighty one and exceedingly bitter. Grant them eternal rest, Lord, and may perpetual light shine upon them.

In paradisum

May the angels receive thee in paradise; at thy coming may the martyrs receive thee, and bring thee into the holy city Jerusalem. May the choir of angels receive thee, and with Lazarus, once a beggar, mayst thou have eternal rest.

Instrumentation

2 Flutes [Flûtes]
2 Clarinets (B♭) [Clarinettes]
2 Bassoons [Bassons]
4 Horns (F) [Cors]
2 Trumpets (F) [Trompettes chrom. en Fa]
3 Trombones
Timpani [Timbales]
2 Harps [Harpes]
Violins I, II [1ers et 2ds Violons]
Violas I, II [1er, 2e Altos]
Cellos I, II [1er, 2e Violoncelle]
Basses [Contrebasse]
Organ [Orgue]

Soprano solo
Baritone solo

Sopranos
Altos
Tenors
Basses

French Terms in the Score

Anches, reeds
choeur, choir
et, and
Fonds, foundation stops, *Fonds de 8 p.,* 8-foot nonreed stops
les, the
pieds, feet
Récit, Récit (manual)
seuls, only
tous, all

REQUIEM IN D MINOR
OP. 48

REQUIEM

I_INTROÏT et KYRIE

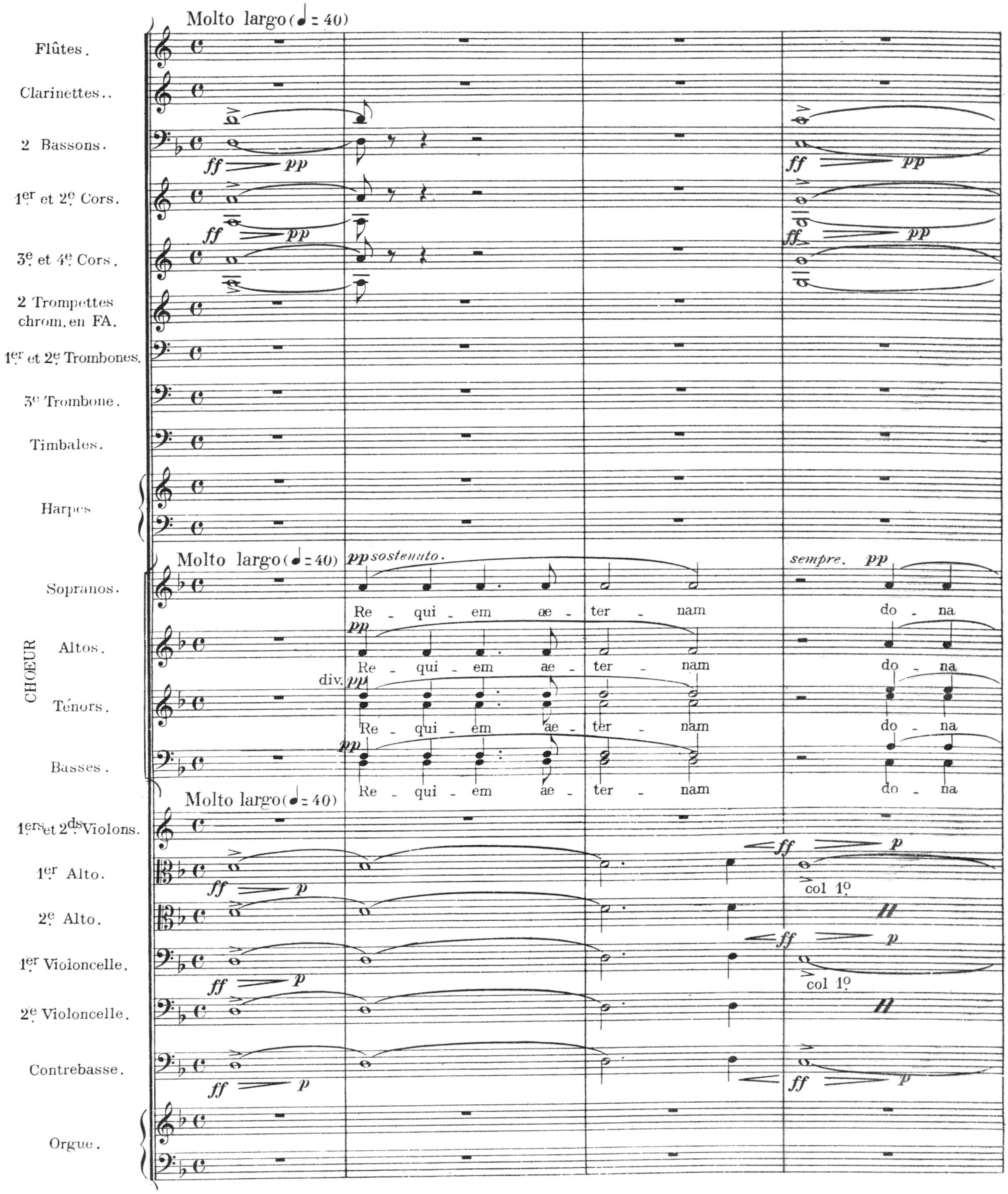

A
sempre.
ff
molto sostenuto.
cresc.
f
e - is do - mi - ne
et lux per - pe - tu - a
p
f sempre.
ff sempre.
molto sostenuto.

ff
2e
ff
3e
pp
dim.
p
lu - ce - at
lu - ce - at
dim.
lu - ce - at
lu - ce - at
dim.
lu - ce - at
lu - ce - at
dim.
p
lu - ce - at
lu - ce - at
dim.
p
sff
div.
dim.
p
sff
dim.
p
sff

B
pp
pp
B
pp
lu - ce - at e - is
ppp
lu - ce - at e - is
lu - ce - at e - is
ppp
lu - ce - at e - is
lu - ce - at e - is
lu - ce - at e - is
pp
lu - ce - at e - is
lu - ce - at e - is
B
p sempre.
unis.
p sempre.
p sempre.

Andte moderato (♩= 72)
Andte moderato (♩= 72)
dolce espressivo.
p
Re - qui - em ae - ter - nam
Andte moderato (♩= 72)
p dolce espressivo.
p dolce espressivo.
p
dolce espressivo.
Fonds de 8 p.
p

C
C
cresc.
f
do - na - e - is do - mi - ne
et lux per - pe - tu - a lu -
C
cresc.
f
cresc.
f
cresc.
f
cresc.
f
cresc.
f
cresc.
f

- ce - at e - is
p dolce
p espress.
p
p
div.
p
p
espress.
p

D
D
dolce.
cresc.
f
re - qui-em ae - ter - nam
do - na
do - na e - is
D
f
f
f
f
f

sempre f
p
do - mi_ne et lux per - pe - tu_a lu - ce - at e-
sempre f
p
sempre f
p
p
p

E
dim.
f
dim.
f
dim.
1ºf
dim.
E
is
E
ff sosten.
dim.
ff sosten.
dim.
p
div.
ff
dim.
Anches et fonds.
f
dim.
Fonds.
legato.
dim.

dolce
p
1º
pp
3e
pp
dolce.
Te de - cet hym - nus De - us in Si - on
p
p
p dolce sempre.
col 1º
dolce.
p sempre.

et ti - bi red - de - tur vo - tum in Je - ru - sa - lem.
cresc.
p
Anches et fonds.

F
1º
p
pp dolce
pp
F ff
ex - au - di ex - au - di o - ra - ti - o - nem me - am
F
col 1º

f
mf
dimin.
ff sempre.
ad te om - nis ca - ro ve - ni - et
ad te om - nis ca - ro ve - ni - et
ad te om - nis ca - ro ve - ni - et
ad te om - nis ca - ro ve - ni - et
ff sempre.
ff sempre.
ff sempre.
ff sempre.

G
1º
dolce.
1º
dolce.
3e
pp dolce.
dim.
om - nis ca - - ro, ve - - ni - et
om - nis ca - - ro ve - - ni - et
om - nis ca - - ro ve - - ni - et
om - nis ca - - ro ve - - ni - et
G
dim.
col 1º.
dim.
dim.
dim.
Fonds seuls.

dolce espressivo.
Ky - ri - e Ky - ri - e Ky - ri - e e -
Ky - ri - e Ky - ri - e Ky - ri - e e -
Ky - ri - e Ky - ri - e Ky - ri - e e -

H
-le - i-son
Kyrie e-le - i-son e-le - i-son e-
H cresc.
f
cresc.
f
H
cresc.
f
cresc.
f
cresc.
f
cresc.
f

1º dolce.
p
pp
pp
p
- le - i - son
Chris - te
Chris - te
Chris - te e -
ff
col 1º
Anches et fonds.

J
p
pp
pp
p
-le - i - son
J sempre p
Chris - te
Chris - te
e - le - i -
-le - i - son
Chris - te
Chris - te
e - le - i -
-le - i - son
Chris - te
Chris - te
e - le - i -
-le - i - son
Chris te
Chris te
e - le - i -
J
p sempre
p
p sempre
p
Fonds seuls.
p

pp
son
e - le - i - son
son
e - le - i - son
son
e - le - i - son
son
e - le - i - son
p
mf
p
pp
mf
p
mf
p
mf

K
1º dolce.
pp
1º.
p e dimin.
pp
K
pp
e - le - i - son
e - le - i - son
e - le - i - son
e - le - i - son
K
col 1º
mf
p
pp
pp sempre al fine.
pp sempre al fine.
p al fine.

pp
e - le - i - son
e - le - i - son
e - le - i - son
e - le - i - son

II_OFFERTOIRE

pp dolcissimo.
O do - mi - ne Je - su chris - te rex
pp
O do - mine Je - su
f sempre.
ff
p
f sempre.
ff
p
f sempre.
f
p

A
A
glo - ri - ae li - be - ra a - nimas de - func - to - rum de poe - nis in - fer -
chris - te rex glo - ri - æ li - be - ra a - nimas de - func - to - rum de poe - nis in - fer -
A
pp
col 1º
pp
pp
p

B
B
B
pp sempre.
_ni ___ et depro_fun _ do la_ _ cu ___ O do_mi_ne Je_su chris_te rex
_ni ___ et depro_fun _ do_la_ _ cu ___ O do_mine Je_su
pp
p
p
p
p

dolce.
glo - ri - æ li - be - ra a - nimas de - func - to - rum de o - re le - o -
chris - te rex glo - ri - æ li - be - ra a - nimas de - func - to - rum de o - re le - o -
pp
pp
col 1º
pp

C
C
C
nis ne abs or be at Tar ta rus O do mi ne Je su chris te rex
nis ne abs or be at Tar ta rus Je su christe
O do mi ne Je su

glo_ri_a ___ O do_mi_ne Je_su chris _ te ___ ne ca_
___ rex glo_ri_a, O do_mi_ne Je _ su chris _ te ___ ne ca_
chris _ te rex glo_ri_a Je_su chris _ te ___ ne ca_

D
D
p
dant
in obs - cu - rum
dant
in obs - cu - rum
dant
in obs - cu - rum
D
f
p
espress.
f
f
p
col 1º
f
f
p
f

Andte moderato (♩ = 63)
Baryt. Solo p dolce.
Hos - ti - as
Andte moderato (♩ = 63)
Andte moderato (♩ = 63)
p
ff
p
pp
div.
p cresc.
ff
p
pp
div.
pizz.
p
dolce.

— et pre - ces ti - - bi do - mi - ne Lau - -

E
cresc.
dis of fe ri mus tu sus ci pe
mf
pizz.

p dolce.
pro a - ni - ma - bus il - lis qua - rum ho - di - e
pp
pp
pp
p

mf
me - mo - ri - am fa - ci - mus
p
mf
pp
arco.
div.
pizz.

F
F
p
fac - e-
F
pp
Solo.
p

as fac e_as do_mi_ne de_mor te tran_si re
dim.
p
pp
pp pizz.

G
G
meno p
ad vi - tam quam o - lim A - bra - hae
G
espressivo.
p
espressivo.
dolce.
arco
pp
p

H
H dim.
pro - mi - sis - ti
pro - mi - sis -
H
espress.
cresc.
f
p
pp
pizz.
arco.
mf

mf
p
ti et se - mi- ni e - jus
mf
pp
mf
pp
arco.
pizz.
mf
pp
mf
p

Iº Tempo adagio molto (♩= 48)
Sopr.
O do_mine Je_su chris _ te rex glo _ ri_
Iº Tempo adagio molto (♩= 48)
pp
O do_mine Je_su chris _ te Je_su chris _ te rex glo _ ri_
pp
O do_mine Je_su chris _ te
pp
O do_mine li_be_
pp
O do_mi_ne Je_su chris _ te rex glo _ ri_ae rex glo _ ri _ ae
Iº Tempo adagio molto (♩= 48)
dolce.

J
cresc.
f
ae li-be-ra a-ni-mas de-func-to-rum de poe-nis in-fer- ni, de poe-nis in-
ae li-be-ra a-ni-mas de-func-to-rum de poe-nis in-fer- ni, de poe-nis in-
ra a-ni-mas de-func-to-rum de poe-nis in-fer- ni, de poe-nis in-
li-be-ra defunc-to-rum de poe-nis in-fer-
pp
col 1º
f
arco.
pizz.

K
dim.
pp
dolce sempre.
K
- fer - ni et de pro - fun - do la - cu Ne ca - dant in obs - cu -
- fer - ni et de pro - fun - do la - cu Ne ca - dant in obs - cu -
- fer - ni et de pro - fun - do la - cu Ne ca - dant in obs - cu -
- fer - ni et de pro - fun - do la - cu Ne ca - dant in obs - cu -
K
p
pp
p
col 1o
arco.
p
p
p

pp
-rum A- -men, a- - -men a- men
-rum A- -men, a- - -men a- men
-rum A- men, a- - -men a- men
-rum A- -men, a- - -men a- men
pp
pp

III_SANCTUS

Andte modto (♩=60)
Flûtes.
Clarinettes.
2 Bassons.
1er et 2e Cors.
3e et 4e Cors.
2 Trompettes chrom. en FA
1er et 2e Trombones
3e Trombone.
Timbales.
Harpes.
pp
Andte modto
Soprano Solo.
CHŒUR
Altos.
Ténors.
Basses.
Andte modto (♩=60)
Sourdines.
1ers et 2ds Violons
1er Alto.
pp
2e Alto.
1er Violoncelle.
2e Violoncelle.
Contrebasses.
Orgue.
pp

pp
Sanc - - tus Sanc - - tus
pp
Sanc - - tus Sanc -
1res Basses. pp
Sanc - - tus Sanc -
pp
pp

Sanc - tus Do - mi - nus
tus
Sanc - tus do - mi -
tus
Sanc - tus do - mi -
pp
pp

A
A
p
do - mi nus de - - us
- nus
p
do - mi - nus de -
p
- nus
do - mi - nus de -
A
pp

p
de - - us Sa - ba - oth
- us
pp
De - - us Sa - ba -
pp
- us
De - - us Sa - ba -
pp

B
B
p
Sanc - tus Do - mi- nus de - us
- oth
- oth
B
p

pp
De - us de - us Sa - ba - oth
pp
De - us de - us Sa - ba - oth
pp
Div.
pp
Pizz.

C
C
sempre dolce.
Ple - ni sunt coe - li et ter - - - ra
C
Div.
sempre
Arco.
pp

sempre dolce
Glo - ri - a Glo - ri - a tu - a
Glo - ri - a Glo - ri - a tu - a
Div.
pp
pp

D
D
Ho - san - na in ex - cel - - - - sis
D
Div.
Div.

F
poco a poco cresc.
ff
hosanna in excelsis
poco a poco cresc.
Unis.

dim.
pp
p
sempre.
ff
Ho - san - na in ex - cel - sis
1ers et 2e Bas.
Col 1o

Iº Solo.
f
dim.
pp
Iº Solo.
pp
dim.
p
dim.
ff
Ho - san - na in ex - cel - sis
in ex - cel - sis.
in ex - cel - sis.
Pizz.
dim.
p
Pizz.
Pizz.

pp
pp
p sempre
p
pp
pp
in ex - cel - - sis
Sanc
pp
Sanc
Div.
pp
Sanc
Div.
pp
Sanc
Arco.
pp
Arco.
Arco.
pp
Arco.
Arco.
pp
pp
sempre.

-tus
-tus
-tus
-tus
dolce.
p

dim.
pp
tr
dim.
pp
dim.
pp

IV PIE JESU

Adagio. (♩= 44)
Flûtes.
Clarinettes.
2 Bassons.
1er et 2e Cors.
3e et 4e Cors.
2 Trompettes chrom. en FA
1er et 2e Trombones
3e Trombone.
Timbales.
Harpes.
Adagio. (♩= 44)
dolce e tranquille
Soprano Solo.
p Pi - e Je - su Do - mi - ne do - na e - is
CHŒUR
Altos.
Ténors.
Basses.
Adagio. (♩= 44)
1ers et 2ds Violons
Sourdines.
1er Alto.
Sourdines.
2e Alto.
Sourdines.
1er Violoncelle.
Sourdines.
2e Violoncelle.
Contrebasses.
Récit. Solo.
8 Pieds.
p dolce.
Orgue.

pp
1º
pp
1º
pp
pp
re - qui_em
do - na
e - is
re - qui_em
pp
Div.
Div.
pp
pp
pp

A
pp
A un poco più
mf
Pi - e Je - su do - mi - ne do - na e - is
A
meno. p

1º p
2º p
3º
2º pp
p
p
dim
re - qui - em do - na e - is Re - qui - em
p
p
p
p
Div.
dim.
p

B
B
dolce
p
do_na e_is do_mi_ne do_na e_is re_qui_em_
B
pp
pp
Unies.
pp
pp
sempre legato.
pp

C
poco cresc.
sem_pi_ter_nam re - qui_em sem - pi_ter - nam re - qui_em
p
pp

D
1º Solo.
p
1º dolce.
p
mf
D
sem - pi-ter - nam re - qui-em
Pi - e Je - su Je - su
D
mf espressivo.
mf
ppp
mf

a 2
dolce. p
dolce. p
dolce.
Pi - e Je - su Do - mi - ne do - na - e - is do - na - e - is

E
1º
pp
poco rit.
sem - pi-ter - nam re - qui-em sem - pi - ter - nam re - qui - em
sempre pp

V AGNUS DEI

Andante. (♩ = 69)
Flûtes.
Clarinettes.
2 Bassons.
1er et 2e Cors.
3e et 4e Cors.
2 Trompettes chrom. en Fa.
1er et 2e Trombones
3e Trombone.
Timbales.
Harpes.
Andante. (♩ = 69)
CHOEUR
Sopranos.
Altos.
Tenors.
Basses.
Andante. (♩ = 69)
1ers et 2ds Violons.
1er Alto.
2e Alto.
1er Violoncelle.
2e Violoncelle.
Contrebasse.
Orgue.
p
p dolce espress.
Col 1o.
Pizz.
poco a poco
cresc.

Tous les Ténors.
p dolce espress.
Ag - nus
f
dimin.
p
p sempre
sempre

De - i qui tol - lis pec - ca - ta mun - - -

A
A
poco cresc.
di do na e is do na e is
A
p
poco cresc.
poco cresc.
poco cresc.
poco cresc.
poco cresc.

B
f
p
3º
dim.
Re - qui - em
Ag - nus
Ag - nus
Ag - nus
Ag - nus
cresc.
Col 1º
Col 1º
Col Vlle
Arco.

de - i Ag - nus de - i qui tol - lis
cresc.

C
p
cresc.
f
sempre
f
pec - ca - ta
mun -
di
do -
na
sempre f
cresc.
sempre
f sempre

1o
p
dim.
do - na e - is re - qui - em
do - na e - is re - qui - em
do - na e - is re - qui - em
espress.
Ag - nus
do - na e - is re - qui - em
p
p
espress.
p
Pizz.
Pizz.
p p Pizz.
p
Solo
p espressivo.

cresc.
de - i qui tol - lis pec - ca - ta mun - di do -
dolce espress.
p
dolce espress.
p
Arco.

D
D
-na do - na e - is re - qui - em
D
p
p
p
p
p

p dolce sempre
Lux
sem - pi - ter - nam re - qui - em
p
Col 1º
Arco.

E
E
ae - ter - na lu - ce - at e - is lu - ce - at
pp
Lux ae - ter - na lu - ce - at e - is
Div.
pp
Lux ae - ter - na lu - ce - at e - is
Div.
pp
Lux ae - ter - na lu - ce - at e - is
E
p dolce
p dolce
p
p
p dolce

e - - is do - mi - ne
dolce sempre
cum sanc - tis
lu - ce - at e - is do - mi - ne
cum sanc - tis
lu - ce - at e - is do - mi - ne
cum sanc - tis
lu ce - at e - is do - mi - ne
cum sanc - tis
sempre dolce
p
p
p sempre dolce
p

pp dolce.
pp dolce.
tu - is in ae - ter - num qui - a pi - us
tu - is in ae - ter - num qui - a pi - us
tu - is in ae - ter - num qui - a pi - us
tu - is in ae - ter - num qui - a pi - us
p

F
pp
cresc.
F
cresc.
molto.
pi - us es cum sanc tis tu - is
pi - us es cum sanc - tis tu - is
pi - us es cum sanc - tis tu - is
pi - us es cum sanc - tis tu - is
F
cresc.
molto
cresc.
Col 1º
cresc.
molto.
cresc.
molto.
cresc.
molto.

mf
f
f sempre
in æ - ter - num qui - a pi -
in æ - ter - num qui - a pi -
in æ - ter - num qui - a pi -
in æ - ter - num qui - a pi -
f sempre
f sempre
f sempre

G
ff
ff sempre
G
us
es
G
ff sempre
ff sempre
ff sempre
ff sempre
f sempre

Molto largo. (♩=40)
ff pp
Molto largo. (♩=40)
pp
Re - qui - em æ -
Re - qui - em æ -
Re - qui - em æ -
Re - qui - em æ -
Molto largo. (♩=40)
ff p
Col 1º
Col 1º
Col Vlle
dolce
pp

H
ff
pp
cresc.
_ter _ nam
do _ na e _ is do _ mi _ ne
Et lux per _
dolce.

sempre
dim.
p
f
dim.
-pe - tu-a lu - ce - at lu - ce - at lu - ce - at
pp
-pe - tu-a lu - ce - at lu - ce - at lu - ce - at
pp
-pe - tu-a lu - ce - at lu - ce - at lu - ce - at
f
pp
-pe - tu-a lu - ce - at lu - ce - at lu - ce - at
sempre ff
sempre ff
dim.
pp
dim.
pp
pp
f
dim.
pp

I.º Tempo. (♩=72)
I.º Tempo. (♩=72)
e - - - - is
e - - - - is
e - - - - is
e - - - - is
I.º Tempo. (♩=72)
p espress.
espress.
H
p
espress.
p
Pizz.
p
dolce.
p espress.

1º
p
dolce
p
pp
dim.
p
f
dim.
p
dim.
p
f
dim.
p
f
p
Arco.
dim.
p
f
dim.
p

VI_LIBERA ME

Moderato (𝅗𝅥 = 60)
Flûtes.
Clarinettes.
2 Bassons.
1er et 2e Cors.
3e et 4e Cors.
2 Trompettes chrom. en Fa.
1er et 2e Trombones.
3e Trombone.
Timbales.
Harpes.
Moderato (𝅗𝅥 = 60)
Baryton Solo.
Li be_ ra me Do _ mi_ne
CHOEUR
Sopranos.
Contraltos.
Ténors.
Basses.
Moderato (𝅗𝅥 = 60)
1ers et 2ds Violons.
1er Alto.
2e Alto.
pizz.
1er Violoncelle.
p
col 1º
2e Violoncelle.
pizz.
Contrebasse.
p
Orgue.
p
stacc

A
A
de mor - te ae - ter - - na
In di - e il - la tre -
A

men - da in di - e il - - - la Quan - do coe - li mo -

B
cresc.
f
sempre.
-ven - di sunt quan-do coe - li mo - ven-di sunt et ter - ra Dum
B
f col 1º
sempre.
cresc.
f
sempre.
cresc.
f
sempre.
cresc.
f
sempre.

Tempo.
sempre f
poco rall.
Tempo.
ve - ne_ris ju_di_ca - _re sae_cu_lum per ig_ _nem
Tempo.
col 1º

C
C
pp
Tre - mens, tre - mens fac - tus sum e -
pp
Tre - mens, tre - mens fac - tus sum e -
pp
pp
Tre - mens fac - tus sum e -
pp
Tre - - - mens e -
C
pp
arco.
pp
arco.
pp
p
p

D
D
cresc.
f
- go et ti - me - o et ti - me - o Dum dis - cus - si - o ve - ne -
- go et ti - me - o Dum dis - cus - si - o ve - ne -
- go et ti - me - o Dum dis - cus - si - o ve - ne -
- go et ti - me - o Dum dis - cus - si - o ve - ne -
D
cresc.
cresc.
f
f

Più mosso (𝅗𝅥 = 72)
attacca
ff
rit at que ven tu ra i ra
p
sempre.

ff
Di - es il - la Di - es i - ræ
ff sempre.
Ca - la - mi - ta - tis
ff
Di - es il - la Di - es i - rae
ff sempre.
Ca - la - mi - ta - tis
ff
Di - es il - la Di - es i - rae
ff sempre.
Ca - la - mi - ta - tis
ff
Di - es il - la Di - es i rae
ff sempre.
Ca - la - mi - ta - tis
ff sempre.
sf
col 4º
col 4º
col Vcelle
f sempre.

E
ff
et mi-se - ri - ae
Di - es il - la Di - es Mag - na
ff sempre.

F
dolce.
mf
p
f
p
F
sempre.
dim.
p
et a ma ra a ma ra val de
Re qui em ae
et a ma ra a ma ra val de
Re qui em ae
p
et a ma ra a ma ra val de
Re qui em ae
p
et a ma ra a ma ra val dc
Re qui em ae
F
p
sf
sf
p
sf
p
p

poco cresc.
p
cres - - cen - do.
- ter - - nam Do - - na e - is Do - - mi-
- ter - - nam Do - - na e - is Do - - mi-
- ter - - nam Do - - na e - is Do - - mi-
- ter - - nam Do - - na e - is Do - - mi-
cresc.
cresc.
cresc.
cresc.

G

mf pp

G

f p

sempre dolce.

p

ne Et lux per - pe - tu - a lu - ce - at

ne Et lux per - pe - tu - a lu - ce - at

ne Et lux per - pe - tu - a lu - ce - at

ne Et lux per - pe - tu - a lu - ce - at

G p dolce.

f p

p dolce.

mf p

H Moderato (𝅗𝅥 = 60)
p
pp
H Moderato (𝅗𝅥 = 60)
e - - - - is
pp
e - - - - is lu - ce - at e -
e - - - - is
pp
e - - - - is lu - ce - at e -
H Moderato (𝅗𝅥 = 60)
pp
pizz.
pp pizz.
pp pizz.
pizz.
pp
stacc.
pp

pp
pp
3e.
mf
is
is
f
f
col 1o.
f
f
f
f
f
mf
f

pp
3e
p dolce.
li - be_ra me Do_mi_ne de mor_te ae_ter_na
p
p sempre.
sempre.

J
J
sempre p
In di - e il - la tre - men - da in di - e il -
3e.
pp
J

K
p
pp
pp
3e
p
pp
pp
mf
cresc.
la
Quan - do coe - li mo - ven - di sunt. Quan - do
la
Quan - do coe - li mo - ven - di sunt, Quan - do
la
Quan - do coe - li mo - ven - di sunt, Quan - do
la
Quan - do coe - li mo - ven - di sunt, Quan - do
f
col 2e V.celle
mf

p
cresc
f
f sempre.
p
cresc
f
f sempre.
f sempre.
coe - li mo - ven - di sunt et ter - ra Dum ve - ne-
coe - li mo - ven - di sunt et ter - ra Dum ve - ne-
coe - li mo - ven - di sunt et ter - ra Dum ve - ne-
coe - li mo - ven - di sunt et ter - ra Dum ve - ne-
f
f sempre.
f
f sempre.
f
f sempre.
f
f sempre.
f
f sempre.

L
p
pp
p
pp
p
pp
p
pp
L
-ris judi-ca - re seculum per ig - nem
-ris ju-di-ca - re se-cu-lum per ig - nem
-ris ju-di-ca - re se-cu-lum per ig - nem
-ris ju-di-ca - re se-cu-lum per ig - nem
L dim.
dim.
dim.
dim.
dim.

Baryt. Solo
p dolce.
p
Li - be - ra me Do - mi - ne De - mor - te ae-
p
p
arco.
p
p
p

pp
ter - na li - be - ra me Do - mi - ne
pp
li - be - ra me Do - mi - ne
pp
li - be - ra me Do - mi - ne
pp
li - be - ra me Do - mi - ne
pp
li - be - ra me Do - mi - ne
arco.
arco.
arco.
arco.
pp

VII. IN PARADISUM

di - - - sum
De - du - cant

A
A sempre
an - ge li in tu - o ad-
A

ven - tu sus - ci - pi - ant te mar - - ty - res

B
sempre dolce
B
et per du - cant te
in ci - vi - ta - tem
B
Pizz.
pp

cresc
sanc - tam Je - ru - - - - sa - lem Je - ru - - - - sa -
Div. Ten. pp
cresc
Je - - - - ru - - - sa - lem
Div. Bass. pp
Je - - - - ru - - - sa - lem
dolce
p
p
Arco.
pp

C
C
ppp
lem Je - ru - - sa - lem Je -
Alti. ppp
Je - ru -
f
Je - ru - sa - lem
Je - - ru
ppp
ru -
dim
pp
mf

Harpes.
ru - sa - lem
sa - lem
sa - lem
sa - lem
dolce
Cho -
dolce sempre
pp dolce sempre
pp
pp sempre

-rus an - ge - lò - - rum te sus-ci-pi-at

D
D
et cum La - za - ro quon - - dam pau - - pe -
D

cresc
cresc
-re
Et
cum
La - - za - ro
quon - - dam
cresc
cresc
p e cresc
cresc

E
pau - pe - re
ae - ter - nam
ha - be - as
Re -
Div.

qui
em
pp
ae
qui
em
qui
em
qui
em
dolce
pp Pizz.

F
F
-ter - - nam ha - - be - as
pp
ae - ter - - nam ha - - be - as
pp
ae - ter - - nam ha - - be - as
pp
ae - ter - - nam ha - - be - as
F
Pizz.

THE END

Dover Opera, Choral and Lieder Scores